AMERICAN LANGUAGE REPRINTS

VOL. 5

AN ANCIENT NEW JERSEY INDIAN JARGON

compiled by
Anonymous

edited by
J. Dyneley Prince

With additional discourses in the jargon
by Gabriel Thomas

STUDIARE · APPLICARE · CREARE

Evolution Publishing
Merchantville, New Jersey.

Reprinted from:

J. Dyneley Prince, 1912. "An Ancient New Jersey Indian Jargon,"
American Anthropologist vol. 14, p.508-524.

with additional material from:

Gabriel Thomas. 1903 (reprint of 1698 edition). *An Account of
Pennsylvania and West New Jersey*. Cleveland:Burrows Brothers.

First Published 1997
Reprinted 2006

Printed in the
United States of America

ISBN 1-889758-83-3

CONTENTS

Preface to the 1997 Edition

The seventeenth century saw the beginning of European colonization along the Delaware River, an area at the time inhabited by Algonquian Indians of the Lenape or Delaware tribe. The necessity of communication between these natives and European colonists inspired the creation of a Delaware pidgin language, today commonly referred to as the New Jersey or Delaware Traders' Jargon.

Though it was based on their native language, this jargon was not used natively among Delawares, who would have used it only for communication with colonists. Some scholars have suggested that it may have also been used with other non-related tribes such as those of Iroquoian descent (Thomason 1980), but this theory has not been widely accepted.

Most of the vocabulary of the Jersey jargon comes from the Southern Unami dialect of Delaware, originally spoken in the Lower Delaware River Valley in modern-day Southeastern Pennsylvania, Southern New Jersey and Delaware. While the jargon itself apparently ceased to be spoken sometime in the 1700's, the Unami dialect upon which it was based continues to be spoken today, though only by a handful of older Delawares in Oklahoma. Thanks to the preservational efforts of these last native speakers and linguists working with them, a number of Unami Delaware courses and instructional materials are now available; particularly useful for the beginning student is a recent treatment (Blalock, Pearson and Rementer 1994).

Nothing in the known jargon grammar can be traced solely to English grammatical influence; there are, however, a number of features which can only be explained from Delaware itself (Thomason 1980), lending credence to the idea that the jargon developed from a conscious simplification of Delaware grammar by the Indians themselves. The original grammatical inflections of the Delaware language, namely its complex verbal prefixing and suffixing, were dispensed with almost entirely in jargon usage, resulting in an over-simplified idiom that was nevertheless adequately suited for treaties and commerce.

The vocabulary reprinted in this volume is ultimately derived from an anonymous manuscript source in the State Archives of New Jersey at Trenton. The manuscript is labeled "The Indian Interpreter" and included in a record book from Salem County; it can probably be dated to 1684. Three subsequent published works drew from this manuscript.

The first reprinting was in the journal *American Historical Record* of 1876, but contained many errors in typography and transcription; a second and better version appeared in William Nelson's *The Indians of New Jersey* in 1894.

The third published version of the vocabulary is the one reprinted here, taken from an article in the *American Anthropologist* of 1912 edited by J. Dyneley Prince. Prince's article is not without a few of its own errors; he omits some words which were printed by Nelson, and a few of his etymologies have turned out on more scrupulous analysis to be incorrect. Nevertheless, these do not detract from the overall value of the article, to date the only word-by-word analysis of the Indian Interpreter vocabulary.

Dr. Prince remarks in his introduction that he finds it strange that Daniel Brinton, who was so thorough in collecting all the various examples of Lenape literature, makes no mention of the Salem Records. In fact, Brinton does refer to the manuscript in his book, though only as a brief note in the appendix, which may explain why Prince did not notice it. Brinton's comments are worth quoting here:

DIALECT OF THE NEW JERSEY LENAPE. (p. 46)

An interesting specimen of the South Jersey dialect of the Lenape is preserved in the office of the Secretary of State, Trenton, N.J. It is a list of 237 words and phrases obtained in 1684 at Salem, N.J. It was published in the *American Historical Record*, vol. I, pp. 308-311, 1872. The orthography is English, and it is evidently the same trader's jargon which Gabriel Thomas gives (See p. 76.) The *r* is frequent; man is *renus leno*; devil is *manitto*; God is *hockung tappin* (literally, "he who is above"). There are several typographical errors in the printed vocabulary.

—D.G. Brinton, The Lenâpé and their Legends, p. 255.

Prince's original article organized the jargon entries numerically to 261, but was not alphabetized: here all his numbers have been done away with in favor of an alphabetical arrangement. The sometimes archaic English spelling of the Indian Interpreter—preserved by Prince—has here been modernized: i.e. *scissors* for *sissors*, *linen* for

3

lynnen, etc. Also modernized are some archaic phrases such as *whither goest thou?* The jargon words, however, are reproduced exactly as Prince transcribed them, and since the anonymous author generally follows English orthographical conventions, the word-forms should present no special problems to the modern reader.

The *Indian Interpreter* is one of the two main sources for our knowledge of this Delaware jargon; another fairly extensive collection of 500 words and phrases was taken down by the Swedish missionary Johannes Campanius in the 1640's and has been reprinted in Volume 3 of this series. There are also shorter jargon vocabularies in the works of Gabriel Thomas, William Penn and Peter Lindeström, and occasional words in a few other texts of the period.

As Gabriel Thomas' recording of the jargon is mentioned by both Brinton and Prince, the latter of whom makes an etymological study of some of it in the introduction, Thomas' *Discourses* have been included as an appendix in this volume. These were first published in his 1698 book *An historical and geographical account of the Province and Country of Pensylvania; and of West New Jersey in America.* The general layout of Thomas' work has been preserved as originally written, in the nature of a jargon dialogue with English translations. His version of the numbers are printed in the table immediately following.

—Claudio R. Salvucci, 1997.

Bibliography and Recommended Reading

Blalock, Lucy, Bruce Pearson and James Rementer. 1994. *The Delaware Language.* Bartlesville, OK:Delaware Tribe of Indians.

Brinton, Daniel G. 1969 [1884]. *The Lenâpé and their Legends.* New York:AMS Press.

Brinton, Daniel G. and Albert Seqaqind Anthony. 1889. *A Lenâpé–English Dictionary.* Philadelphia:The Historical Society of Pennsylvania.

Goddard, Ives. 1995. "The Delaware Jargon". in *New Sweden in America.* Hoffecker et al., eds. pp. 137-149. Newark:University of Delaware Press.

Goddard, Ives. 1996. "Pidgin Delaware". in *Contact Languages: a Wider Perspective.* Sarah G. Thomason, ed. Amsterdam:Benjamins.

Nelson, William. 1894. *The Indians of New Jersey.* Paterson, NJ:The Press Printing and Publishing Company.

Pearson, Bruce L. 1988. *A Grammar of Delaware: Semantics, Morpho-Syntax, Lexicon, Phonology.* Dewey, OK:Touching Leaves Indian Crafts.

Thomas, Gabriel. 1903 [1698]. *An Account of Pennsylvania and West New Jersey.* Cleveland:The Burrows Brothers Company.

Thomason, Sarah Grey. 1980. "On Interpreting 'The Indian Interpreter'". *Language in Society* 9:167-193.

Introduction

While at Trenton as Acting Governor of New Jersey in 1912, the writer found in the vaults of the Department of State an old manuscript volume of deeds, pertaining to Salem county, N.J.[1] In this collection, inserted next to a deed bearing the date 1684, is "The Indian Interpreter", a list of 261 words and phrases in the English of the period and in a mixed dialect of the New Jersey Delaware language, the arrangement being at random with no attempt at alphabetical order. The material given in this list was published without comment in Lossing's *Historical Record* (vol. 1, 1872, pp. 308-311), but so faultily, with so many misunderstandings of the original orthography, and with such a quantity of typographical errors, that the reproduction is of no service whatever to students of the Lenâpe. The writing in the manuscript is somewhat difficult to read for one accustomed only to modern script. Thus, there are many ambiguous characters, such as the similar capitals *S-L* and *R-K*, and the almost identically written minisculæ *n-r-v-s; l-h*, etc., so that a person entirely unacquainted with Lenâpe could hardly hope to make even an approximately correct transcription of the Indian words.

The list is of considerable philological interest, first, because it undoubtedly represents a Traders' Jargon, used between the Delaware River whites and the Indians, almost grammarless and based chiefly on English construc-

---

[1] Salem Surveys, No. 2; stiff paper, yellow with age, in original leather binding.

tion, like the Chinook and Eskimo traders' idioms of the North; and secondly, because the Delaware material, broken and erroneous as it often is, is not entirely Minsi. There can be no doubt that we have here Unami and Unalachtigo elements as well as Minsi. The following instances should be compared: *nahaunum* 'raccoon'; *miningus* 'mink'; *copy* 'horse'; *s* for *sch* in *singkoatam*; *s* for *tsch* in *singa* 'when'; *r* for *l* in *ruti* 'good'; *raamunga* 'within'; *rhenus* for *leno* 'man'; *roanonhheen* 'northwest wind', none of which words or peculiarities is of northern origin.[1]

Strangely enough, Brinton, in his Lenâpé and their Legends, makes no mention of this manuscript material in the Salem Records, although he knew of and commented briefly on the Traders' Jargon.[2] The jargon of the Salem Records and that given by Thomas are identical. save that the former source is much fuller than the few specimens cited by Thomas.[2]

The jargon words given by Thomas, which are not found in or are noticeably variant from the language of the Salem Records, are comparatively few and as follows:[3]

---

[1] Cf. J. D. Prince, The Modern Minsi Delaware Dialect, *Amer. Journ. of Philol.*, XXI, pp. 295-302.

[2] Op cit., pp. 75 ff. as instanced by Gabriel Thomas in his *History and Geography; Account of the Province and Country of Pennsylvania and West New Jersey in America*, London 1698, a still accessible reprint of which appeared in New York in 1848.

[3] The following abbreviations have been used in this paper: B. = Brinton, *Lenâpé–English Dictionary*, Philadelphia 1888; Z. = Zeisberger's *Indian Dictionary*, printed from original manuscript, Cambridge 1887; Pass. = Passamaquoddy; Aben. = Abenaki; A. = Albert Seqaqkind Anthony, collaborator with Brinton in his *Lenâpé–English Dictionary*;

apeechi, *quickly* = SR √ **hapicha**.

aroosise, *old* = Z. **mihilúsis** old man, from stem = decay.

benoin(g)tid, *boys*; not a plural = Del. **pilwin**, young (**pil**) one (**win**) + the dim. √ **-tit**. Note the interchange of l and n, Unalachtigo fashion.

beto, *fetch* = SR. **petto**.

chekenip, *turkey*; Unalachtigo form (Brinton, "Lenâpé", p. 37) = SR. **sickenom**.

chase, *skin* = SR. **hayes**. Palatalization of Del. **ches**. See below s.v. **kachi**.

chetena, *strong* = Z. **tschítanne**, hard; **ntschítannessi**, I am strong.

enychan, *children*; not a plural = Z. **nitschaan**, my child; Aben. and Pass. **nijan**.

etka, *or* = **etek**, where it may be; used like the Germ. **sei**; Fr. **soit** for 'or'.

haloons, *shot* = SR. **alluns**.

hayly, *very* = B. **cheli**, 'much'.

hita, *friend*; cf. SR. **netap**.

hodi, *farewell* = Eng. **howdy**.

kabay, *horse* = SR. **copy**.

kachi, *how many* = Z. **kechi**; B. **keechi**. This guttural

---

RW. = Roger Williams; SR. =Salem Records; OA. = Old Abnaki; P. = Prince. It should be noted that the phonetic system followed by the writer of the Salem Record is that of the English of the seventeenth century. Both Brinton and Zeisberger followed the German method of notation, with certain irregularities on the part of Brinton.

must have been pronounced with a strong palatalization to be represented by English **ch!** Cf. 'below', **marchkec**.

koon, *winter* = SR. **coon**.

marchkec, *red* = Z. **mechksitschik**, 'red ones'.

megis, *sheep* = SR. **mekis**.

mogy, *yes* = SR. **mochee**. Note the use of g in Eng. for the palatal sound.

moos, *cow* = SR. **muse**.

(kee) namen, *you see* = Z. **nemen**; common Algonquian stem.

neskec, *blue*, *black*; B. **nescalenk** or **nesgessit lenâpe**, 'black men'.

nowa = Aben. **nawa**, a resumptive particle like Eng. 'now' at the beginning of a phrase.

ochqueon, *coat* = SR. **aquewan**. Was this palatal ch or a guttural? Most probably the latter owing to Dutch influence (?) on the notation.

opeg, *white* = SR. **sepeck**.

peo, *he will come* = SR. **payo**; **poh**.

squatid, *girls*. Not a plural; **squa(w)**, on which see SR. **squaw** + dim. **-tit**.

tongtid, *young* = Z. **tangeto**, little; B. **tangiti** + dim. √ **-tit**.

(nee) weekin, *I live, dwell* = Z. **wik**, house; common Algonquian **weesyouse**, meat = SR. **iwse**.

Perhaps the most interesting phonetic feature of this jargon, of which the present paper gives all that is extant, is the interchange of *r* and *l*. It will be observed that the writer of the Salem manuscript gives *rhenus* and *leno* for 'man'; *ruti* and *olet* for 'good', showing that, even as early as 1684, the whites could hardly distinguish between the Indian *r* and *l*. The *r* was no doubt similar to the old Aben. *r* of Rasles' Dictionary, which is now everywhere represented by *l*, and also to the Iroquois *r* which is at present beginning to become *l* on the St. Regis reservation in northern New York; i.e., the old Delaware *r* was a thick palatal which permitted a ready permutation to both *l* and *n*, as was the case in Unalachtigo (Brinton, Lenâpé, p. 38, and see just above s.v. *benoin(g)tid*. It should be observed, in studying the following comparisons, that both Brinton and Zeisberger used the German system of notation in writing the Lenâpe.

JERSEY JARGON — ENGLISH

Abij, *water*; Z. **m'bi**; B. **mbi**; Aben. **nebi**.

Accoke, *a snake*; B., Z. **achgook**; Aben. **skok**.

Acotetha, *apple*; must be the same stem as Z. **achquoací-lennees** 'blackberries'; no doubt a misapplication. Both B. and Z. give **āpel** for 'apple'.

Ahalea coon hatta, *have abundance of snow, hail, ice*; **ahalea** = B. **allowiwi** 'more'. **Coon** = Z. **guhn** 'snow' (see **whinna**).

Alloppan, *tomorrow*; Z. **alappa**; A. **ajappa**.

Alloquepeper, *cap, hat*; B., Z. **alloquepi**.

Aloppan, *tomorrow*; cf. **alloppan**.

Alunse, *lead*; B. **alluns** 'arrow' (A. first 'arrow'; then 'bullet'). Proper word for 'lead' was **tákachsin** 'soft stone' (P.).

Anna, *mother*; perhaps a jargon word. The proper Del. was B. **gahowes**; Z. **gahowees**.

Aquewan, *coat, cloak,* or *woolen cloak*; B. **achquiwanis** 'blanket'; Z. **achquiwanes**.

Aquittit, *little girl*; B. **ochque-tit**; lit. 'little woman'. Ignores guttural.

Assin, *stone, iron, brass*; i.e. anything hard (P.); B. **achsin**; Z. **achsün**. In Del. 'iron' was **sukachsin** 'black stone' (P.); Z. **sukachsün**.

Assinnus, *kettle, pot*; a jargon word from **assin** 'stone, iron,' etc.; B., Z. **hoos** 'kettle'.

Attoon attonamen, *going to look for a buck*; **attoon** = Z. **achtu** 'deer'. This word probably is concealed in the modern corrupt form **Tuxedo** which the Marquis de

Chastellux in 1785 translated 'there are plenty of deer'; i.e. **Tuxedo** possibly = **achtuhuxítonk** = B. **achtuhu** 'there are many deer' + **-xit** 'where one gets them' + the loc. **-onk** = 'place where one gets many deer'. **Attonamen** is from **naten** 'go after something'. The form should be **n'naten** 'I seek him' (anim.); (n)**attonamen** is inanimate and wrong here.

Bee, *water*; Z. **m'bi**; B. **mbi**; Aben. **nebi**.

Brandywyne, *rum*; proper word; **lilenowokgan**; Z.

Cakickan, *perch*; I cannot place. Perhaps should be read **cakielan**, same stem as B. **machkalingus**; Z. **moechkalingus** 'sun-fish' (?).

Ceet, *the foot*; B. **w'sit**; **w'chsiit**.

Checonck, *looking-glass, mirror*; The usual expression was B., Z. **pepenaus** 'mirror', from **pipinamen** 'differentiate, choose'. The Natick word for 'mirror' was **pepenautchitchunkquonk**; Narr. **pebenochichauquánick** 'the thing by which one sees a reflection'. **Checonck** of the jargon ms. seems to contain the final element of a Del. word akin to these long combinations just indicated.

Chingo ke matcha, *when will you go?* **tschinge** 'when'; cf. **singa**.

Cochmink, *without*; B. **kotschemunk**; Z. **kotschmunk**; Pass. **kotchmek**.

Cockoon, *stockings*; B., Z. **gagun**.

Cohockon, *mill*; B. **tachquahoakan**; Z. **tachquoahoácan**.

16

Coon, *snow*; Z. **guhn**. (see **whinna**).

Copohan, *sturgeon*; RW. **kauposh**; Aben. **kabasa**; connected with Z. **copachcan**, 'thick, stiff'. Note OA. **kabasse**, 'closed in'; same stem as Del. **kpahhi**, 'close'; see **poha**.

Copy, *horse*; I cannot place. The proper word was B. **nenajungus**; Z. **nechnajungees**. **Kabay** is given by Thomas (see above Introduction).

Cothtingo, *a year*; B. **gachtin**; Z. **gachtün**. Note the rendering of the guttural in the jargon by 'th'. Cf. **noeck**.

Cuttas, *six*; B. **guttasch**; Z. **guttaasch**.

Cuttas quing quing, *six ducks*; cf. **quing quing**.

Cutte, *one*; B. **ngutti**; Z. **gutti**. The *n* is inherent; cf. Pass. **neqt**, 'one'.

Cutte gull, *one gilder*; sixpence.

Cutte hatta, *one buck*; lit. '(I) have one'; 'buck' = **ajapeu**; B. and Z.

Cutte steepa, *one stiver*; Dutch stuiver.

Cutte wickan cake, *one fathom of wampum*; cf. B. **newo wikan** 'four fathoms'.

Haas, *eight*; B., Z. **chaasch**.

Hamo, *shad*; I cannot place; B., Z. **schawanámmek**.

Hannick, *squirrel*; Z. **anicus** 'fence-mouse' = 'ground squirrel' or 'chipmunk'.

Hapitcha, *by and by*; Z. **pecho**; B. **apitschi**.

Hapockon, *pipe*; Z. **hopoacan**; **achpiquon**. A. "archaic".

Haxis, *old woman*; corruption of Z. **chauchschiessis**.

Hayes, *skin (not dressed)*; B. **ches**; Z. **choy**.

Hickole, *yonder*; Z. **ikalísi**; B. **ika talli.**

Hickott, *the legs*; Z. **wickaat.**

Hickywas, *the nose*; Z. **wickíwon**; B. **wikiwon.**

Himbiss, *cloth, linen*; cf. Z. **hembsigawan,** 'tent'; lit. 'a cloth dwelling'; or 'where one dwells in cloth' (**wig** 'dwell').

Hitock, *a tree*; Z. **mehíttuk.**

Hitock nepa, *there stands a tree*; Z. **nípu** 'he stands'.

Hoccus, *fox*; Z. **woakus** 'gray fox'. Note the mod. N.J. placename **Hohokus,** still translated "many foxes". This is probably an abbreviation of **hôkusak** 'foxes'.

Hockcung, *a chamber*; lit. 'on the ground'; cf. **hockung kethaning.** B. gives **wikwamtit** 'chamber'; lit. 'little (**-tit**) house'.

Hockehockon, *plantation*; Z. **hakihácan.**

Hocking, *the grounds*; Z. **hacki**; B. **haki** 'earth'; lit. 'in the earth'. Cf. Pass **ki**; Aben. **a'ki,** etc.

Hockung kethaning, *up the river*; B. **kittan** 'great (tidal) river'. The last element **-tan** is the same as that seen in **manhattan** = **m'na'tan** 'an island surrounded by tidal water' = **-tan.** The word **hockung** must have meant 'down (the river)', as it = **hakink** 'on the earth, down, under'. Upstream = **nallahiwi,** B.

Hockung tappin, *God's*; lit. 'on earth (**hockung**) is God' (**tappin** = Pass. **tepeltek**; Aben. **tabaldak** 'lord').

Hoppenas, *turnips*; B. **hobbin** 'potato'; Z. **hobbenis** 'turnip', with dim. **-s.**

Hosequen, *corn*; Z. **chasqueem**; B. **mesaquem** 'ear of c.'

Hosquen, *corn*; Z. **chasqueem**; B. **chasquem**.

Hunnikick, *otter*; B. and Z. **gúnamochk**.

Husco lallacutta, *I am very angry*; seems to mean 'irritated'; Z. **lalha** 'scrape'; B. **lalhan**. Properly 'angry' was B. **manunxin**.

Husco matit, *it is very ugly*; Z. **machtit** 'ugly'.

Husco seeka, *it is very handsome*; B. and Z. **husca** 'very'; Z. **schiki** 'handsome'.

Husko opposicon, *much drunk*.

Husko purso, *very sick*; **purso** = B. **palsin**; same stem seen in **tespahala**.

Husko taquatse, *it is very cold*.

Hwissameck, *catfish*; B. **wisamek** (A. = 'fat fish'; archaic; at present **wahlheu** 'mud-fish'); Z. **wíssameek**.

Iough matcha, *get gone*; lit. *now go*; **iough** = B. **juke** 'now'; cf. **iucka**; **matcha** 'go depart'; cf. **tacktaugh matcha**, **tana ke-matcha**.

Iough undoque, *go yonder*; lit. *'now there'*; cf. **iucka**.

Issimus, *a brother*; should probably be connected with Pass. **nsiwes** 'my brother'. This is the same stem seen in Z. **schiess** 'uncle'. Z. gives **nimat, kimat** 'my brother, your brother'.

Itcoloha, *a cradle*; for Z. **tchallan** 'Indian bedstead'; wrongly, **tschallaan** in B.

Iucka, *day, a day*; really B. **juke** 'now'; **juke gischquik** 'today'. Cf. **iough matcha**.

Iwse, *I use meat* or *flesh*; really *meat*; B. **ojoos**; Z. **ojos**.

Kacko pata, *what have you brought?*; B. **peton**; Z. **pêtoon** 'fetch'. Note the absence of the personal prefix.

Kake, *wampum*; Z. **gequak**; B. **gock.**, but A. (Mod. Del.) **keekq**.

Kako meele, *what will you give for this?* The root **mil** is common Algonquian for 'give'; cf. Pass. **ke'kw k'mîlin wechi ni** 'what will you give me for this'?

Ke cakeus, *you are drunk*; Z. **achkienchsu** 'a drunken man'.

Kecko gull une, *how many guilders for this?* On **kecko**, see below; **gull** 'guilder'; Dutch **gulden**.

Kecko kee hatta, *what do you have?* B. **olhatton**, 'have, possess'. Cf. nr. 194.

Kecko kee wingenum, *what will you have?* **kecko** = Z. **köcu**; B. **kolku** 'what, something'. The root **wing-** appears in B. **winginamen** 'delight in'; Z. **wingilendam**; Aben. **n'wigiba-losa** 'I should like to go', etc.

Kecko lwense, *what is your name?* Really = *'his name'*. B. **lüwunsu** 'he is called'; Aben. **liwizo**; Pass. **w't-lēwis**. Cf. **keeko kee lunse une**.

Keck soe keckoe kee wingenum, *'say what hast thou a mind to'*. The **-soe** is clearly identified with the indefinite Pass. **-ws** in **ke'kws** 'what, anything'.

Keeko kee lunse une, *what do you call this?* Note **keeko**; should probably be read **kecko** (cf. **kecko kee wingenum**); **kee** = 2 p. sing.; on **lunse**, see **kecko lwense**.

Kee mauhulome, *will you buy?* Z. **mahallammen**; B. **mehallamen** 'buy'. Cf. **me mauholumi**.

Keenhammon, *grind it*; B. **kihnhammen**.

Kee wingenum une, *do you like this?*; **une** = B. **won** 'this'.

Ke husko nalan, *you are very idle*; Z. **nolhandowoagan** 'idleness'; B. **nolhand** 'lazy'.

Ke kamuta, *no, I did not steal it*; see **matta**.

Ke manniskin une, *will you sell this?* The stem **mahal** = 'sell'; cf. Z. **na** (sic! = **ne-**) **mahallamagentsch** 'I will sell it'. In Aben., however, **manahômen** = 'sell'; clearly same stem as here.

Ke runa matauka, *you will fight*; quite a wrong transla- tion: **ke runa** = **kiluna**, the incl. 'we'. The plural 'you' would have been **kiluwa**; 'you' = **ke-**.

Kins kiste, *a maid ripe for marriage*; corruption of **choanschikan** 'virginity'.

Kishquecon, *a week*; B. **gischquik**.

Kisho, *a month*; B., Z. **gischuch** 'month'.

Kis quicka, *this day*; *a day*; B. **gischquik**; Z. IDEM.

Kitthaning, *river*; B. **kittan**; see **hockung kethaning**. **Kitthaning** is locative 'at the river'.

Kush-kush, *hog*; B. and Z. **goschgosch**; onomatapoeia.

Lamiss, *fish*; B. **names**; Z. **namees**.

Leecock, *table, chair, chest*; evidently from **liechen** 'lie down'; Z. **liwíchin** 'rest'. Apparently a jargon word (?).

Leno, *man*; B. **lenno**.

Linqwes, *wild cat*; Z. **tschinque**. In the Minsi of the north, a form similar to the Pass. **lox** 'wolverine' must have existed, as we find the word **kātelôs** for 'wild cat' in Jersey Dutch (Prince, op. cit., p. 484).

21

Loan, *winter*; Z. **lowan**; B. **loan**. Cf. **roanonhheen**.

Locat, *flour* or *meal*; B. **lokat**; Z. **lócat**.

Mack, *boar*; I cannot place; B. gives **welchos** 'stallion, boar'. It is possible that the writer meant to write **wack** which might be a corruption of **welchos**.

Makees, *sheep*; B. **mekis**, onom. from **memekis** 'bleat'.

Maleema cacko, *give me something*; **mil** 'give' (see **nee meele**); the form should be **milil** 'give me'; Aben. **milin**.

Mamadowickon, *peach* or *cherry*; I cannot place.

Mamanhiikan, *peach* or *cherry*; I cannot place.

Mamolehickon, *book* or *paper*; B. **mamalekhikan** 'writing, letter' (A. "in crooked lines or stripes"); from **lekhammen** 'write'.

Manadickon, *peach* or *cherry*; I cannot place.

Manitto, *the Devil*; B. **Manitto** (A. 'spirit'); cf. Z. **manittowáhalan** 'bewitch'.

Matcha pauluppa shuta, *I have caught a buck*; B. **palippawe** 'buck' and Z. **tchunásu** 'catched' from which **shuta** is obvious. The entire phrase means 'I am going (**matcha**; cf. **tacktaugh matcha**, for **nee matcha**) a buck to catch'.

Match poh, *he is come*; *coming*. This use of **match-** to denote the present action is common in Aben. and Pass. Note Z. **peu** ('he comes'.

Matta, *no*; B. and Z. **matta** 'no, not' = the neg. **atta** with **m**-prefix.

Matta ne hatta, *I have nothing*; B. **matta** 'no, not'. Cf. **matta**.

Matta olet, *it is bad*; lit. 'it is not good'.

Matta ruti, *it is good for nothing*; **matta** 'not'; **ruti = luti =** the stem **wul-** + the neg. **-i**.

Meelha, *the hair*; Z. **milach**; pl. **milchall**.

Me matta wingeni, *I don't care for it*; note the Eng. **me** in the jargon for Del. **ne-ni** and also the neg. **-i**.

Me mauholumi, *I will buy it*; again Eng. **me** as above; Z. **mahallammen**; B. **mehallamen** 'buy'. The **-i** here may be a relic of the 1 p. **-i** = 'I will buy it for myself' (?).

Mesickecy, *make haste*; schauwessin; Z. **schauwessi**; probably **mesickecy** is for **wesickecy**, a corruption of the **-wessin** element in the above words (?).

Mets, *eat*; Z. **mizin**; and cf. Aben. **mits** 'eat'.

Minatau, *a little cup to drink in*; **men** is a common Algonquian stem 'to drink'; B. **menachtin** 'drink together'.

Miningus, *a mink*; Z. **winingus**. This seems to show the derivation of the Eng. **mink**; Swed. **mänk** from the Delaware dialects.

Minne, *drink* or *ale*; B. **menen** 'drink'; **menewagan** 'drinking'; Z. **menewoacan** 'drink' (n.).

Mitchen, *victuals*; B. **mizewagan**; Z. **mizewoagan**.

Mitthurrus, *husband*; must = **witthullus** 'her husband'; same stem as in B. **allewussowagan** 'majesty, supremacy'. Cf. **qualis**.

Mochee, *ay, yes*; Z. **moschiwi** 'clearly'; Z. gives **bischi** 'yes, indeed'.

Mockerick accoke, *rattlesnake*; lit. 'big [see **mockorick**] snake'. Z. **wischalowe** = 'rattlesnake' (= 'frightener'; A.).

Mockorick, a *great deal* = B. **mechakgilik** 'great'; **macheli**; **mecheli** 'more'.

Moholo, *a canoe*; B. **amochol**; Z. **amóchol**.

Momolicomum, *I will leave this in pawn*; must contain root **mol**, seen in Z. **wulatschi-mol-sin** 'treat about peace'.

Munockon, *(?) or a woman*; manuscript indistinct. This is probably B. **allamachtey** 'womb, inward parts' (?), and denotes the pudendum feminæ.

Muse, *cow*; B. **mos**; now = 'deer' and 'elk' (A.).

Mwes, *elk*; B. **mos**; Z. **moos**.

Nacking, *the hand*; B. **nachk**; properly 'my hand'.

Nahaunum, *raccoon*; Z. **náchenum**. The Minsi word was **espan** (cf. A. in Brinton), a word which still lives in the Jersey Dutch of Bergen County **häspân**; cf. J. D. Prince, The Jersey Dutch Dialect, Dialect Notes, vol. III, part vi, p. 479.

Necca, *three*; B., Z. **nacha**.

Necka couwin, *after three sleeps*; *3 days hence*; Z. **gauwin** 'sleep' (cf. **quequera qulam tanansi...** etc.)

Neckaleekas, *hen*; seems onom. The nearest equivalent is B. **quekolis**; A. **wékolis**, 'whip-poor-will'. Mod. Del. **kikipisch**; Z. **gigibis**; probably a reduplication of the Dutch **kip(pen)**, 'chicken(s)'.

Ne dogwatcha, *I am very cold*; *I freeze*. With these words, cf. B. **tachquatscho** 'he is cold, shivering'; Z. **tachquatschúwak** 'they freeze' (see **whinna**).

Nee hatta, *I have*.

Nee meele, *I will give you*; should be **k'milen**, Z.; cf. Aben. **k'milel**. Cf. **maleema cacko**.

Nee tukona, *my country*; from **hacki**; viz., n of the 1 p. + the intercalated **-t-** before a vowel or soft h + the element **uk-ak = hacki**.

Ne hattunum hwissi takene, *I will go hunting in the woods*; in two lines in the ms. With **ne hattunum hwissi**, cf. Z. **ndochwilsi** 'I go hunting'. The usual root is **allauwi**; cf. J. D. Prince, "The Modern Minsi Delaware Dialect," Amer. Journ. of Philol., XXI, pp. 294-302. 'In the woods' was properly **tékenink**; B., Z. **tékene**.

Ne holock, *anus?*; English not given in the manuscript; probably meant 'my hole' and was construed as 'arse-hole'; hence, the modest writer of the ms. left the English blank. The regular Del. word for 'arse-hole' was **saputti**; cf. J. D. Prince, "Dying American Speech Echoes from Connecticut," Proc. Amer. Philos. Soc., XLII, p. 351. Cf. **ne olocko toon**.

Ne mathit wingenum, *we will be quiet*; really *'I will be quiet'*; **mathit** must be a corruption of Z. **clammieche** 'be still, lie quiet'; B. **klamachpin** (?). Note the apparent use of **wingenum** 'wish', for the future. The jargon reproduces the guttural by th; cf. **noeck, cothtingo**.

Ne maugholame, *I bought it*; B. **mehallamen**; see **me mauholumi**.

Ne olocko toon, *we run into holes*; verb-form, really 1 p. pl. excl. from Z. **woalac**; B. **walak**; A. **waleck** = 'a hollow, excavation; not a hole which penetrates'.

25

Neshas, *seven*; B. **nischasch**; Z. **nischâsch**. The -**asch** element corresponds to the -**ôz** of the Aben. in **nguedôz**, 'six'; **tôbawôz**, 'seven'. It must have denoted 'five', as **guttasch-nguedôz**, 'six' = 'one', plus -asch-ôz; i.e. the first element is **gut-ngued** = Pass. **neqt**, 'one'; while **nischasch-tôbawôz**, 'seven' = **nisch** and Aben. **tôba-**, Pass. **taba**, 'two', + -**asch-ôz**; viz., 'one and five', 'two and five', etc.

Netap, *friend*; really *'my friend'*; cf. Pass. **nitap, kitap** 'my, thy f.' The full phrase here in the ms. seems to be **hiyotl netap** 'good be to thee friend', or 'thou good friend'. This **hiyotl** appears to be a part of the verb 'to be' = **hiyp**; cf. **yu** in Aben. and Pass. 'it is', and probably the root of **wul-** 'good'. The sentence is indistinct.

Ne taulle ke rune, *I will tell you*; verb-form from stem **öl**; cf. Z. **kt-öl-len** 'I tell you'. Here in the jargon they used the 1 p. + 3 p. **ne taulle** = **nt-öl-e**; lit. 'I tell him,' and added **ke runa** = **kiluna**; see **ke runa matauka**.

Neuwa, *four*; B., Z. **newo**.

Ne wingenum, *I have a mind to*.

Ninnenuggus, *mare*; Z. **nechnaungési ochquechum** = 'horse female'.

Nippinge, *summer*; really 'next summer'; B., Z. **nipen**.

Nisha, *two*; B. **nischa**; Z. **nischi**.

Nissinach, *twenty*; Z. **nischinachke**.

Noa, *come here*, *come back*; Probably from B. **nawochgen** 'follow', seen also in the resumptive **nawa**.

Noeck, *father*; Z. **nooch** 'my father'; **ochwall** 'his father', etc. Note the hardening of the guttural and cf. **cothtingo, passica catton**.

Nonackon, *milk*; I do not believe there ever was a Delaware word for 'milk'. This word in B. = **nonagan**; Z. **nunagan** 'nipple, mamma'.

Nonshuta, *doe*; B. and Z. **nunschetto**.

Nupane, *the ague*; lit. 'it comes again'; B. **nohenopenowágan** 'the sickness which recurs again' (A.).

Nutas, *bag, basket*; B. **menutes**; the ending -**notey** occurs in Z. **hembinotey** 'bag of linen'. This **nt**- root is seen in Pass. **b'snud**; Aben. **abaznoda** 'basket', lit. 'a wooden bag' (Pass. **epus**; Aben. **abazi** = 'wood, tree').

Oana, *a path, highway*; B., Z. **aney**. See **tana matcha ana**.

Olet, *it is good*; B. and Z. **wulit**.

Opposicon, *beyond yourself* = *drunk*. Probably = B. **achpussin** 'broil, roast'; here = **achpussikan** 'he broils him; he is broiled'; slang (?).

Ouritta, *plain*; *even*; *smooth*. This is simply **wulita** 'it is good', specially applied to land here. Properly 'plain' was B. **memgukek** (A. **schimgek**).

Palenah, *five*; B. **palenach**; Z; Z. **palénachk**.

Papouse, *a suckling child*; a jargon word from the Natick, as **squaw**. Del. was B. **nonetschik**; Z. **nohulentschik** 'children'.

Passica catton, *a half year*; B., Z. **pachsiwi** 'half' + **catton** = B. **gachtin**; Z. **gachtün**. Here the guttural is ignored in the jargon. Cf. **noeck**.

Payo, *to come*; B. **paan**; Z. **peu** 'he comes'.

Penaesit, *boy*; for **penae-tit** = B. **pil-wessin** 'be a boy' (see peray). The ending **-tit** is diminutive.

Pentor, *the ear* or *hearing* = **k'pentol** 'I hear you'; B. **pendamen** 'hear'; Z. **necama k'pendak** 'he hears you'.

Peray, *a lady* = **pelay**; same element as in Pass. **pil-** 'young', seen in Pass. **pil-skwessis** 'young woman, girl'. **Peray-pelay** really means 'young female'.

Pescunk, *nine*; B. **peschgonk**; Z. **peschgunk**.

Piackickan, *gun*; B. **paiachkikan**, 'gun'; lit. 'one fires it off'; from **paiach-kammen** 'fire off'. Contains Eng. 'fire' = **paia**; cf. Chinook Jargon word **piah** 'fire'. The consonant f is foreign to many Indian languages.

Pishbee, *small beer*; Z. **mbîl** 'beer'. Contains the root **-bi** 'water'.

Pocksucan, *knife*; A. **pachschikan**.

Poha, *shut*; B. **kpahi**; A. **kpahhi**; Pass. **k'baha**.

Pomee, *grease, fat*; B. **pomih**; Z. **pomi**.

Ponacka, *the hands*. I cannot explain the prefix.

Pone, *bread*; B. an Z. **achpoan**; B. **nd-apponhe** 'I make bread.' This word survives in the American South for 'corn-bread'.

Poneto, *let it alone*; Z. **ponih** 'leave off, let it alone'; B. **ponemen** 'let go, leave off'. Cf. Pass. **pon'mont'hāg'n agwed'nuk** 'put the paddle in the canoe'.

Poquehero, *it is broke*; B. **poquihilleu**.

Powatahan, *a pair of bellows*; an inversion of Z. **putawoágan**.

Punck, *powder*; B. **ponk** 'dust' (A. 'ashes, powder'); Z. **atta neponggomiwi** 'I have no powder'.

Purso, *sick*; = B. **palsin**. Cf. **husko purso**.

Qualis, *a master*; **k'welis** 'thy master' from **allewus**, as in **mitthurrus**.

Quaquangan, *the neck*; Z. **ochquecanggan**.

Quash matta diecon, *why did you lend it?* B. and Z. **quatsch** 'why'; note Z. **k'nattemihi** 'lend me'. The ms. form must be for **k'nattadikon** 'he lends it to you'; cf. Aben. **k'mil'gon** 'he gives it to you'.

Quequera qulam tanansi oke cowin kee catungo, *where I look for a place to lie down and sleep, for I am sleepy.* This phrase appears on three lines in the ms. and was thus copied by Lossing. The sentence seems hopelessly corrupted, probably by the original scribe. I can find nothing to indicate what was meant by the words **quequera qulam tanansi**, except by supposing that in **tanansi** we have some form of the stem seen in **ndoniken** 'he seeks me'. **Oke** is 'and' = **woak**, cf. **tellen oak cutte**. **cowin** 'sleep' = Z. **gauwin**; cf. **necka couwin**. The words **kee catungo** = 'you are sleepy' and not 'I', as above. They were either wrongly introduced here, or else the whole phrase should be in the 2 p. It may be noted that the q in **quequera** and **qulam** may be indications of the 2 p. = k.

Quing quing, *duck*; B. **quiquingus**. Onom.

Quippeleno, *hoe*; B. **achquipelawon**.

Raa munga, *within*; Z. **allamunque. raa-m** = **lam** in Aben. and Pass. **lami** 'within, inside'.

Rena moholo, *a great boat or ship*; perhaps for **lina(quot) amochol** 'it is like a canoe' (?).

Renus, *man* = **lenno**; see **leno**. The **-s** here is diminutive.

Roanonhheen, *a northwest wind*; Z., B. **lowanáchen** 'north wind'; lit. 'winter wind'; cf. **loan**.

Runcassis, *cousin*; B. **longachsiss** 'cousin', but A. = 'nephew'.

Ruttehock, *the ground will burn and be destroyed*; B., Z. **lúteu** 'it burns'; **haki** 'earth'.

Sackutackan, *breeches*; Z. **sackutáckan**; B. **chessachgutackan** 'leather br.'

Sawwe, *all*; Pass. **m'siu**; Aben. **m'ziwi**. The proper Del. word was B. **wemi**; Z. **weemi**.

Scunda, *the door*; Z. **esquande** = **Eingang**.

Seckha, *salt*; Z. **sikey** (A. "archaic").

Sehacameck, *eel*; B. **schachamek**; Z. **schachameek** (lit. 'it is a straight one').

Seppock, *shoes*; root appears in Z. **nemach-tschipachquall** 'Indian shoes'.

Sepussing, *creek*; diminutive locative of **sipo** 'river'; Aben. **sibo**.

Sewan, *wampum*; perhaps Z. **schejeek**; B. **schejek** 'string of w.' (A. 'edge, borer').

Shamahala, *run*; B. **kschaméhellan** 'fast'.

Shauta, *tobacco*; B. **kschatey**.

Sheek, *grass or any green herb* (should be **skeek**); B. **askiquall, skiquall**; Z. **masgik**; B. **maskik**. Cf. Pass. **m'skí'kwul** 'grasses'.

Sickenom, *turkey*; B., Z. **kaak**, wild goose. A. (**kaág**).

(B. C.) Sickomeele, *(B. C.) will give me so much for it*. Z. **ta-uchtendchi** = 'how much'? A. **keechi** 'how much'. The **si-** element must be the **chi** in **keechi; komeele = k'mîli** 'you give me'. The correct translation is probably '(B. C.), how much will you give me'?

Sickquim, *the spring*; B., Z. **siquon**; Z. **siequangge** 'next spring'; Pass. **siguak** 'in spring'.

Singa, *when*; Z. **tschinge**.

Singa kee natunnum, *when will you fetch it?* Z. **tschinge** 'when'; B. **naten** (A. 'go after something'); Z. **n'natammen** 'I will fetch'.

Singa kee petta, *when will you bring it?* Z. **pêtoon**, 'bring'.

Singa mantauke, *when we fight*; **tschinge** 'when' (see also **chingo ke matcha**); B. **machtagen**; Z. **machtágeen** 'fight'. There is no indication of person in this phrase.

Singkoatum, *I do not care; I will cast it away*; B. **schingattam** ' be unwilling, disapprove'.

Singuap hockin hatta, *'be quiet, the earth has them; they are dead'*. Earth = Z. **hacki**; B. **haki**. Cf. **hatta** 'have'. The **-in** may be for the loc. **-ing, ink**.

Singuope, *hold your tongue*; perhaps a corruption of B. **samuttonen** 'close the mouth'. The proper word was **tschitgussín** (Z.) = 'be silent'.

Skinch, *eye*; Z. **wuschking**; B. **wuschgink** 'eye'; cf. Natick **skizucks**.

Squaw, *a wife*; a jargon word from the Natick **squaw** 'woman'. The kindred Del. was B. **ochque**; Z. **ochqueu**.

Steepa, *farthing* = *stiver*.

Suckolan cisquicka, *a rainy day*; B. **sokelan** 'it rains'; Z. **socelantsch** 'it will rain'; Aben. **soglôn** 'it rains'.

Tackomen, *where did you come from?* = **ta** 'where' + **k**, 2 p. + **omen** 'come from'; cf. Z. **tacúmen**, same meaning.

Tacktaugh matcha, *where are you going?*; Z. **matchil** 'go home'; but in Pass. **mach, maj** is the common root 'to go'. **Tacktaugh** = **ta** 'where' + **k** = 2 p. + **ktaugh**, same element seen in Pass. future **kti**.

Tacockquo, *the fall*; B. **tachquoak**.

Take, *freeze*; B. **taquatten** 'frozen'; **taquatschin** 'freeze'.

Tana hatta, *when did you have it?* **Tana** 'whither' = Pass. **tan** 'what, where, when'.

Tana kee natunum, see **singa kee natunnum**.

Tana ke-matcha, *where are you going?* Cf. Pass. **tan** 'where, whither'. Cf. **taune maugholame**. **Tana** = 'when'.

Tana ke wigwham, *where is your house?* B. **wikwam**; **wiquoam**.

Tana matcha ana, *where goes the path?* B. **aney** 'road, walking road, path'. Cf. **oana**.

Taune kee hatta, *where did you have it?* On **taune** see **tana ke-matcha**; on **hatta**, see **kecko kee hatta**, **singuap hockin hatta**.

Taune maugholame, *where did you buy it?* see **tana ke matcha**; **me mauholumi**.

Tellen, *ten*; B., Z. **metéllen.**

Tellen oak cuttas, *sixteen*; not given by Z.

Tellen oak cutte, *eleven* = *ten and* (oak) *one*; Z. **attach gutti**; i.e., attach = 'more'; it denotes '-teen'. Cf. **quequera qulam tanansi...** etc.

Tellen oak haas, *eighteen*, Z. **attach peschgunk.**

Tellen oak necca, *thirteen*; Z. **tellet woak nacha; attach nacha.**

Tellen oak neshas, *seventeen*, not given by Z.

Tellen oak newwa, *fourteen*; Z. **attach newa.**

Tellen oak nishah, *twelve*; Z. **tellet woak nische; attach nische.**

Tellen oak pallenah, *fifteen*; Z. **attach palénach.**

Tespahala, *smallpox*; B. **despehellan;** Z. **despéhelleu.** Stem is **pa(h)al, pehel** 'be sick' seen in B. **pal-sin (husko purso).**

Tocosheta, *pair of scissors*; contains root of B. **kschikan** 'knife'.

Tollemuse, *servant*; **w't-allemus** 'he hires (sends) him'; cf. B. **allogagan** 'servant'; Z. **allogáman** 'he is sent'. Is **allum** 'dog' from this stem? Cf. Aben. **w'd-alemos** 'his dog'.

Tomohickan, *ax*; Z. **t'mahican;** B. **temahikan.**

Tomoque, *beaver*; B. **ktemaque;** Aben. **tama'kwa.**

Tumaummus, *hare*; Z. **tschemammus.**

Tungshena, *open*; Z. **ntunkschememen,** I open it; B. **tenktschechen; tonktschenemen.**

Twn, *the mouth*; B., Z. **wdoon.**

Undoque, *yonder (little way)*; B. **undachqui** 'whereabouts'; **undach** 'here, this way'. (**A. B.**) **Undoque**, *yond of (A. B)*.

Undoque matape, *sit yonder*; Z. **bemattachpil** 'sit'.

Virum, *grapes*; both B. and Z. **wisachgim**; probably should read **visum** (?).

Weeko, *suet, tallow*; B. **wikul** 'fat in animal's belly'; Z. **wikull**.

Wepeckaquewan, *a white match-coat*; the element **wepeck** 'white' = B. **wapsu** 'white'; Z. **woapsu**. "Matchcoat" meant 'leather coat'; Z. **machtschi-lokees** = 'leather string'.

Wheel, *the head*; Z. **wihl**; B. **wil**.

Whinna, *snow, hail*; Z., B. **wineu** 'it snows'; same stem seen in Z. **guhn** 'snow' (see just below). **Whinna** cannot mean 'hail', which was **tachsigin**.

Wippet, *the teeth*; Z. **wipüt**; B. **wipit**.

Wotigh, *the belly*; B. **wachtey**.

ENGLISH — JERSEY JARGON

Afraid, we are much, *ne rune husco hwissase.*

Ague, *nupane.*

Ale, *minne.*

All, *sawwe.*

Angry, I am very, *husco lallacutta.*

Apple, *acotetha.*

Ax, *tomohickan.*

Bad, *matta olet.*

Bag, *nutas.*

Basket, *nutas.*

Beaver, *tomoque.*

Beer, small, *pishbee.*

Bellows, a pair of, *powatahan.*

Belly, *wotigh.*

Boar, *mack.*

Boat, a great, *rena moholo.*

Book, *mamolehickon.*

Boy, *penaesit.*

Brass, *assin.*

Bread, *pone.*

Breeches, *sackutackan.*

Bring, when will you bring it, *singa kee petta.* **What have you brought**, *kacko pata.*

Broken, it is, *poquehero.*

Brother, *issimus.*

Buck, *attoon.* **Going to look for a buck**, *attoon attonamen.*

Burn, the ground will burn, *ruttehock.*

Buy, will you, *kee mauhulome*. **I will buy it**, *me mauholumi*. **I bought it**, *ne maugholame*. **Where did you buy it**, *taune maugholame*.

By and by, *hapitcha*.

Call, what do you call this, *keeko kee lunse une*.

Canoe, *moholo*.

Cap, *alloquepeper*.

Care, I do not, *singkoatum*. **I don't care for it**, *me matta wingeni*.

Catch, I am going to catch a buck, *matcha pauluppa shuta*.

Catfish, *hwissameck*.

Chair, *leecock*.

Chamber, *hockcung*.

Cherry, *mamanhiikan, mamadowickon, manadickon*.

Chest, *leecock*.

Child, a suckling, *papouse*.

Cloak, *aquewan*.

Cloth, *himbiss*.

Coat, *aquewan*. **Matchcoat, white**, *wepeckaquewan*.

Cold, I am very, *ne dogwatcha*. **It is very cold**, *husko taquatse*.

Come, to, *payo*. **Come here**, *noa*. **Come back**, *noa*. **He is coming**, *match poh*. **From where did you come**, *tackomen*.

Corn, *hosequen, hosquen*.

Country, my, *nee tukona*.

Cousin, *runcassis*.
Cow, *muse*.
Cradle, *itcoloha*.
Creek, *sepussing*.
Cup, *minatau*.

Day, *iucka*. **This day**, *kis quicka*. **A day**, *kis quicka*.
Devil, the, *manitto*.
Drink, *minne*.
Drunk, *opposicon*. **Very drunk**, *husko opposicon*. **You are drunk**, *ke cakeus*.
Doe, *nonshuta*.
Door, the, *scunda*.
Duck, *quing quing*. **Six ducks**, *cuttas quing quing*.

Ear, *pentor*.
Eat, *mets*.
Eel, *sehacameck*.
Eight, *haas*.
Eighteen, *tellen oak haas*.
Eleven, *tellen oak cutte*.
Elk, *mwes*.
Even, *ouritta*.
Eye, *skinch*.

Fall, the, *tacockquo*.
Farthing, *steepa*.
Fat, *pomee*.

Father, *noeck.*

Fathom, *wickan.* **One fathom of wampum,** *cutte wickan cake.*

Fetch, when will you fetch it, *singa kee natunnum, tana kee natunum.*

Fifteen, *tellen oak pallenah.*

Fight, we will fight, *ke runa matauka.* **When we fight,** *singa mantauke.*

Fish, *lamiss.*

Five, *palenah.*

Flour, *locat.*

Foot, *ceet.*

Four, *neuwa.*

Fourteen, *tellen oak newwa.*

Fox, *hoccus.*

Freeze, *take.* **I am freezing,** *ne dogwatcha.*

Friend, my, *netap.* **Good be to you friend,** *hiyotl netap.*

Girl, little, *aquittit.*

Give, I will give you, *nee meele.* **Give me something,** *maleema cacko.* **What will you give for this,** *kako meele.* **How much will you give me,** *sickomeele.*

Go, now, *iough matcha.* **Where do you go,** *tacktaugh matcha; tana ke-matcha.* **When will you go,** *chingo ke matcha.*

God on earth, *hockung tappin.*

Good, *olet.* **Not good,** *matta olet.* **It is good for nothing,** *matta ruti.*

Goose, *kahacke.*

Grapes, *virum.*

Grass, *sheek.*

Grease, *pomee.*

Great, a great deal, *mockorick.*

Grind it, *keenhammon.*

Ground, *hocking.*

Guilder, *gull.* **One guilder**, *cutte gull.* **How many guilders for this**, *kecko gull une.*

Gun, *piackickan.*

Hail, *whinna.* **Have an abundance of hail**, *ahalea coon hatta.*

Hair, *meelha.*

Hand, my, *nacking.* **The hands**, *ponacka.*

Handsome, very, *husco seeka.*

Hare, *tumaummus.*

Haste, make haste, *mesickecy.*

Hat, *alloquepeper.*

Have, I, *nee hatta.* **I have nothing**, *matta ne hatta.* **I have one**, *cutte hatta.* **What do you have**, *kecko kee hatta.* **What will you have**, *kecko kee wingenum.* **When did you have it**, *tana hatta.* **Where did you have it**, *taune kee hatta.* **Say what you have a mind to**, *keck soe keckoe hee wingenum.* **I have a mind to**, *ne wingenum.*

Head, *wheel.*

Hearing, *pentor.*

Hen, *neckaleekas.*

Herb, green, *sheek*.

Hoe, *quippeleno*.

Hog, *kush-kush*.

Hole, *holock*. **My hole**, *ne holock*. **We run into holes**, *ne olocko toon*.

Horse, *copy*. See also **mare**.

House, where is your house, *tana ke wigwham*.

Hunting, I will go hunting in the woods, *ne hattunum hwissi takene*.

Husband, *mitthurrus*.

Ice, an abundance of, *ahalea coon hatta*.

Idle, you are very, *ke husco nalan*.

Iron, *assin*.

Kettle, *assinnus*.

Knife, *pocksucan*.

Lady, *peray*.

Lead, *alunse*.

Leave it alone, *poneto*.

Legs, *hickott*.

Lend, why did you lend it, *quash matta diecon*.

Like, do you like this, *kee wingenum une*.

Linen, *himbiss*.

Looking-glass, *checonck*.

Maiden ripe for marriage, *kins kiste*.

Man, *renus, leno.*

Mare, *ninnenuggus.*

Master, *qualis.*

Matchcoat, white, *wepeckaquewan.*

Meal, flour, *locat.*

Meat, *iwse.*

Milk, *nunackon.*

Mill, *cohockon.*

Mind, I have a mind to, *ne wingenum.* **Say what you have a mind to**, *keck soe keckoe hee wingenum.*

Mink, *miningus.*

Mirror, *checonck.*

Month, *kisho.*

Mother, *anna.*

Mouth, *twn.*

Name, what is his, *kecko lwense.*

Neck, *quaquangan.*

Nine, *pescunk.*

Nineteen, *tellen oak pescunk.*

No, *matta.*

Nose, *hickywas.*

One, *cutte.*

Open, *tungshena.*

Otter, *hunnikick.*

Paper, *mamolehickon.*

Path, *oana*. **Where goes the path**, *tana matcha ana*.

Pawn, I will leave this in pawn, *nomolicomum*.

Peach, *mamanhiikan, mamadowickon, manadickon*.

Perch, *cakickan*.

Pipe, *hapockon*.

Plain, *ouritta*.

Plantation, *hockehockon*.

Pot, *assinnus*.

Powder, *punck*.

Quiet, be. *singuope.* **We will be quiet**, *ne mathit wingenum.*
  Be quiet, the earth has them; *singuap hockin hatta.*

Raccoon, *nahaunum*.

Rainy day, *suckolan cisquicka*.

Rattlesnake, *mockerick accoke*.

River, *kitthaning*. **Up the river**, *hockung kethaning*.

Rum, *brandywyne*.

Run, *shamahala*.

Salt, *seckha*.

Say what you have a mind to, *keck soe keckoe hee
  wingenum*.

Scissors, pair, *tocosheta*.

Sell, will you sell this, *ke manniskin une*.

Servant, *tollemuse*.

Seven, *neshas*.

Seventeen, *tellen oak neshas*.

Shad, *hamo.*

Sheep, *makees.*

Ship, *rena moholo.*

Shoes, *seppock.*

Shut, *poha.*

Sick, very, *huscko purso.*

Sit yonder, *undoque matape.*

Six, *cuttas.*

Sixpence, *cutte gull.*

Sixteen, *tellen oak cuttas.*

Skin, undressed, *hayes.*

Sleeps, after three sleeps, *necka couwin.* **Where I look for a place to lie down and sleep, for I am sleepy**, *quequera qulam tanansi oke cown kee catungo.*

Smallpox, *tespahala.*

Smooth, *ouritta.*

Snake, *accoke.* **Rattlesnake**, *mockerick accoke.*

Snow, *whinna; coon.* **Have an abundance of snow**, *ahalea coon hatta.*

Spring, the, *sickquim.*

Squirrel, *hannick.*

Steal, you have stolen it, *ke kamuta.* **No, I did not steal it**, *matta ne kamuta.*

Stiver, *steepa.* **One stiver**, *cutte steepa.*

Stockings, *cockoon.*

Stone, *assin.*

Sturgeon, *copohan.*

Suet, *weeko.*

Summer, *nippinge.*

Table, *leecock.*

Tallow, *weeko.*

Teeth, *wippet.*

Tell, I will tell you, *ne taulle ke rune.*

Ten, *tellen.*

Thirteen, *tellen oak necca.*

Three, *necca.*

Tobacco, *shauta.*

Tomorrow, *alloppan, aloppan.*

Tongue, hold your, *singuope.*

Tree, *hitock.* **There stands a tree**, *hitock nepa.*

Turkey, *sickenom.*

Turnips, *hoppenas.*

Twelve, *tellen oak nishah.*

Twenty, *nissinach.*

Two, *nisha.*

Ugly, very, *husco matit.*

Very, *husco.*

Victuals, *mitchen.*

Wampum, *kake, sewan.* **One fathom of wampum**, *cutte wickan cake.*

Water, *abij, bee.*

Week, *kishquecon.*

What, *kecko.*

When, *singa; tana.*

Where, *tana.*
Why, *quash.*
Wife, *squaw.*
Wild cat, *linqwes.*
Wind, a northwest, *roanonhheen.*
Winter, *loan.*
Within, *raa munga.*
Without, *cochmink.*
Woods, *takene.*
Woman, *munockon?* **Old woman**, *haxis.* **Maiden ripe for marriage**, *kins kiste.*
Womb, *munockon?*

Year, *cothtingo.* **A half year**, *passica catton.*
Yes, *mochee.*
Yonder, *undoque, hickole.* **Go yonder**, *iough undoque.* **Yond of A.B.**, *A.B. undoque.*

Numerical Table
(Salem Records)

1. Cutte	11. Tellen oak cutte
2. Nisha	12. Tellen oak nishah
3. Necca	13. Tellen oak necca
4. Neuwa	14. Tellen oak newwa
5. Palenah	15. Tellen oak pallenah
6. Cuttas	16. Tellen oak cuttas
7. Neshas	17. Tellen oak neshas
8. Haas	18. Tellen oak haas
9. Pescunk	19. Tellen oak pescunk
10. Tellen	20. Nissinach

DISCOURSES IN THE
INDIAN JARGON

Excerpt from Gabriel Thomas' Account of Pennsylvania and West New Jersey

As to the manner of their Language, it is high and lofty, with a Short Sentence. Their way of counting is by Tens, as to say Two Tens, Three Tens, Four Tens, Five Tens, &c.

I shall now proceed to show something of the manner and way of Discourse that happens between them and Neighbouring Christians that use to deal and traffick with them, or when they meet one another in the Woods accidentally, one looking for his Cattel, and the other a Hunting the Wild Deer, or other Game, by way of Questions and Answers. I shall put the *Indian* Tongue on one side of the Leaf, and the *English* just opposite. Their Discourse is as followeth.

Hitah takoman? *Friend, from where do you come?*

Andogowa nee weekin. *Yonder. My house.*

Tony andogowa nee weekin? *Where yonder? Where is your House?*

Arwaymouse. *Arwaymouse,* (which is the name of an Indian town).

Keco kee hatah kee weekin? *What have you got in your house?*

Nee hatah huska wees youse og huska chetena chase og huska orit chekenip. *I have very fat venison, and good* *strong skins, with very good turkeys.*

Chingo kee beto nee chase og youse etka chekenip.
When will you bring me skins and venison, with turkeys?

Hatopa etka nisha kishquicka. *Tomorrow, or two days from now.*

Keco kee hata kee weekin? *What do you have in your house?*

Nee hata orit poonk og huska horit haloons etka neskec og marchkec ochqueon. *I have very good powder, and very good shot, with red and blue matchcoats.*

O huskia orit. *Very well.*

Kee namen neskec kabay og marchkec moos etka opeg megis? *Did you see black horses and red cows, with white sheep?*

Mata namen megis nee namen neskec kabay undogwa tekany. *I saw no sheep. I did see black horses yonder in the woods.*

Kee namen marchkec moos undogwa tekeny? *Did you see red cows yonder in the woods?*

Mogy. *Yes.*

Kee squa og enychan hatah? *Do you have a wife and children?*

Mogy. *Yes.*

Kacha hatah? *How many do you have?*

Neo. *Four.*

Benoingtid etka squatid? *Boys or girls?*

Nisha benointid og nisha squatid. *Two boys and two girls.*

54

Tongtid enychan hatah? *Do you have a young child?*

Mogy. *Yes.*

Etka aroosise? *How old?*

Neo kishow. *Four months.*

Etka aroosise kee? *How old are you?*

Pelenacheenckan katingan aroosis. *Fifty years old.*

Hodi hita nee huska a peechi, nee, machi Pensilvania huska dogwachi, keshow a peechi nowa, huska hayly, chetena koon peo. *Farewell friend, I will very quickly go to Pennsylvania, very cold moon will come presently, and very great hard frosts will come quickly.*

Numerical Table
(from Thomas)

1. Kooty
2. Nisha
3. Nacha
4. Neo
5. Pelenach
6. Kootash
7. Nishash
8. Choesh
9. Peskonk
10. Telen
20. Nishinchkan
30. Nachinchkan
40. Neochinchkan
50. Pelenchinchkan &c.

Also available:

The Complete American Language Reprint Series on CD-Rom
www.evolpub.com/ALR/ALRCDRom.html

and

The Interactive ALR: An Online, Interactive Database
of Historic Native American Vocabularies and Word Lists
www.evolpub.com/interactiveALR/home.html

Volumes in the ALR series

For more information on the series, see our website at:
www.evolpub.com/ALR/ALRbooks.html

The ALR Supplement Series

Evolution is proud to announce a new series in the preservation of American Indian languages. The ALR Supplement series provides an arena for the publication of large, comprehensive works from the golden age of American philology—many of which have already furnished material for the original ALR series. Reprinting valuable compendia that span several languages, time periods, or culture areas from a time when linguistic data collection was regarded as an integral part of scientific exploration, each of these titles is a treasure trove of American Indian linguistic data, often featuring dozens of languages and dialects and drawing from both printed as well as manuscript and oral sources. Some of these titles have not been reprinted at all since their original appearance but are cited even today as pioneering studies in the comparison and classification of American Indian languages.

Volume 1

Synopsis of the Indian Tribes Albert Gallatin, 1836

A monumental compendia on Native American languages, Gallatin's *Synopsis* is packed with invaluable information on some 81 tribes. The volume commences with four sections of introductory matter giving an overview of the history of the various North American tribes. Section five covers general observations on social and cultural practices and Section six begins an in-depth discussion of Indian languages. Nearly half of this volume is taken up with a massive Appendix dedicated to grammatical notices and vocabularies from dozens of tribes. Of particular note is the Comparative Vocabulary of Fifty-Three Nations which presents a 60-page table of Native translations of common English words. Also included is a further comparison of 16 Native languages and several short miscellaneous wordlists. In bringing together dozens of languages from a vast array of printed and manuscript sources, this volume is a must have for the serious student of American Indian languages.

due October 2006 ~ 430 pp. ~ paperback ~ ISBN: 1-889758-80-9 ~ $39.95

www.ingramcontent.com/pod-product-compliance
Lightning Source LLC
Chambersburg PA
CBHW022031090426
42739CB00006BA/380